/97

D0118715

Elephants Swim

by Linda Capus Riley

illustrated by Steve Jenkins

Houghton Mifflin Company
Boston · New York 1995

Text copyright © 1995 by Linda Capus Riley
Illustrations copyright © 1995 by Steve Jenkins

All rights reserved. For information about permission to reproduce
selections from this book, write to Permissions, Houghton Mifflin
Company, 215 Park Avenue South, New York, New York 10003.

Manufactured in the United States of America

Book design by David Saylor
The text of this book is set in 30-point Albertus Medium.
The illustrations are paper collage, reproduced in full color.

HOR 10 9 8 7 6 5 4 3 2 1

Library of Congress Cataloging-in-Publication Data
Riley, Linda Capus
Elephants swim / by Linda Capus Riley ; illustrated by
Steve Jenkins.   p.   cm.
ISBN 0-395-73654-4
1. Swimming—Juvenile literature. [1. Animal swimming.]
I. Jenkins, Steve, ill. II. Title.
QP310 . S95R55   1995
591 . 1' 852–dc20 94-42185   CIP   AC

To my father, Richmond Riley, who loves elephants

−L. C. R.

For Tyler

−S. J.

Elephants swim with their trunks held high.

Kangaroos swim, but their babies stay dry.

Platypuses use their tails like rudders.

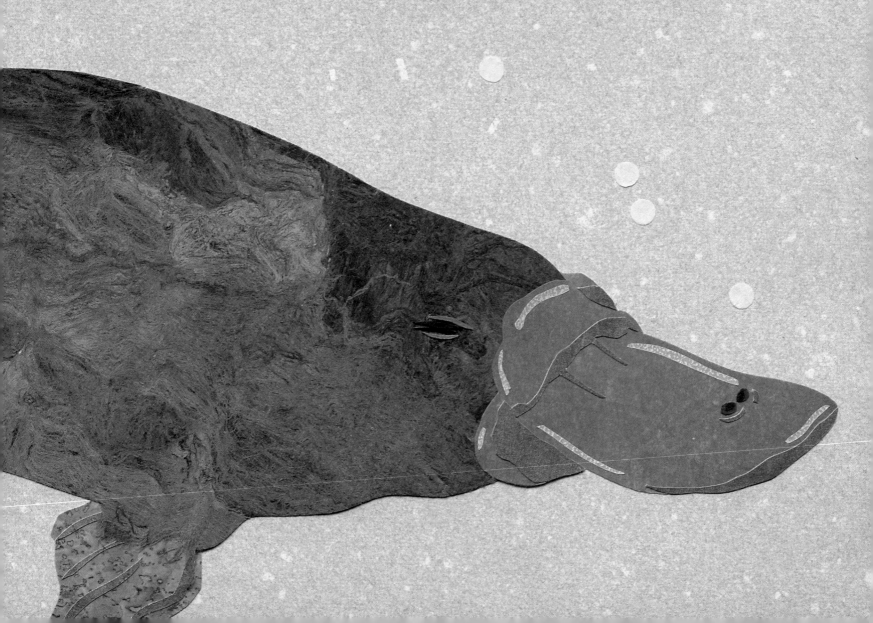

Armadillos walk along under the water.

Tigers swim to get out of the heat.

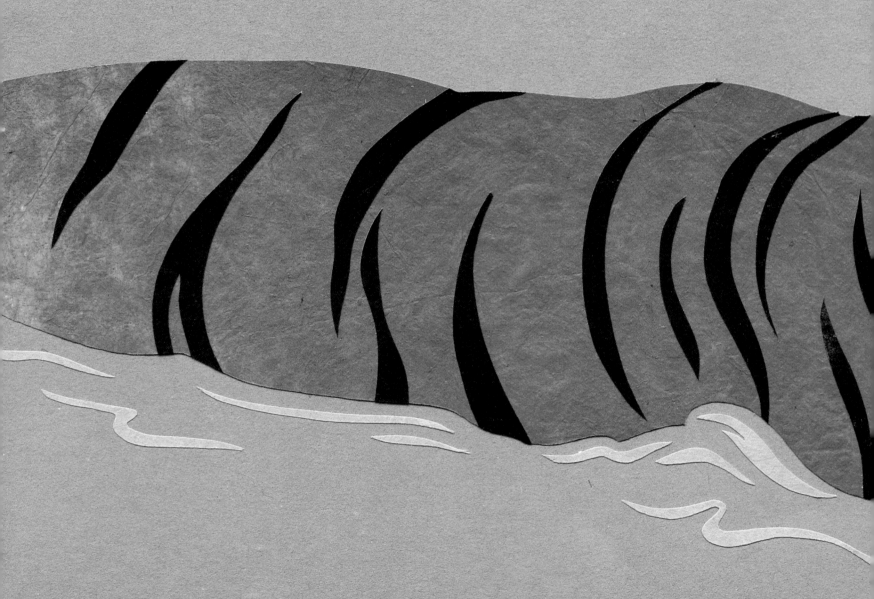

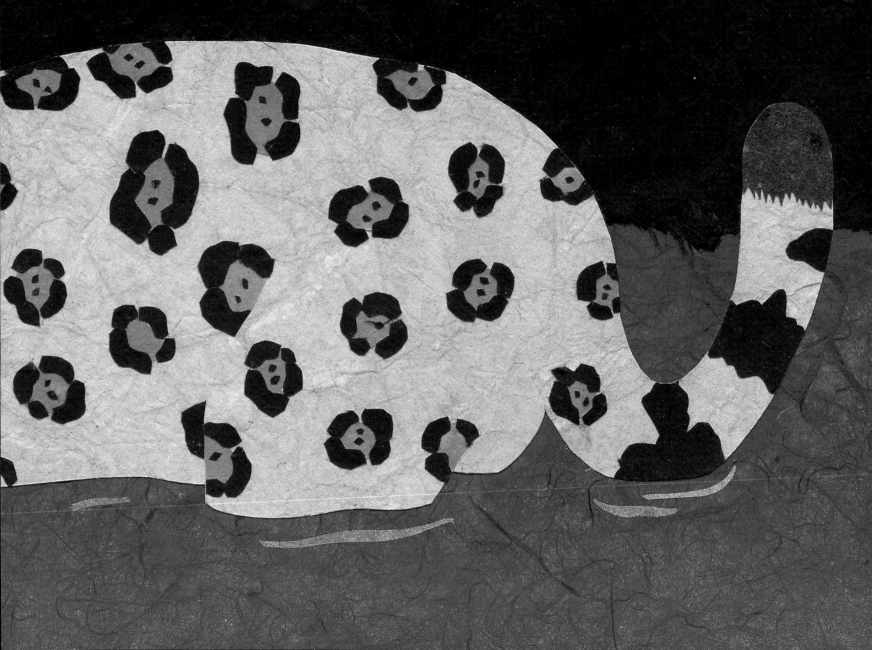

Jaguars scoop up fish to eat.

Sea otters sleep in a cradle of kelp.

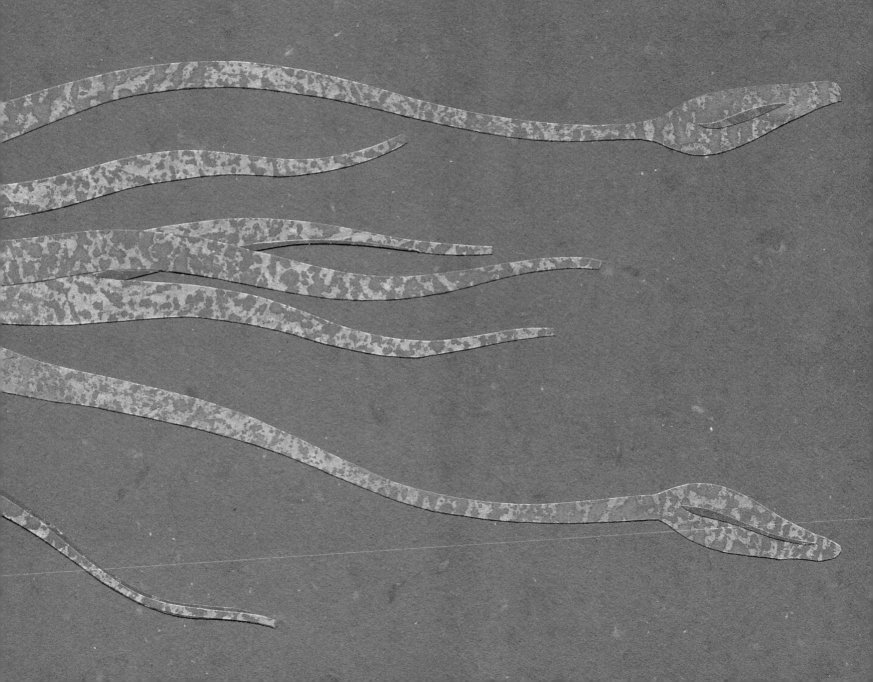

Squid swim backwards, jet-propelled.

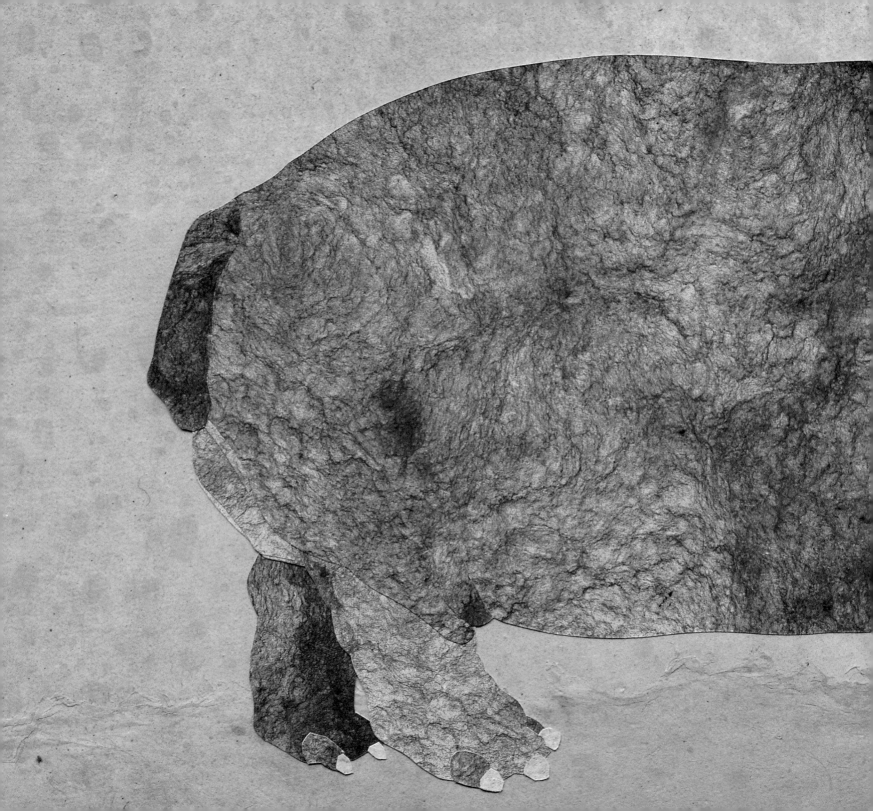

Hippos sink to the bottom to sleep.

ALBUQUERQUE ACADEMY
LIBRARY

Wildebeests wade where the water's not deep.

Pelicans plunge straight down from the sky.

Caribou glide with their heads held high.

Polar bears paddle with the greatest of ease.

Sea turtle babies run straight to the seas.

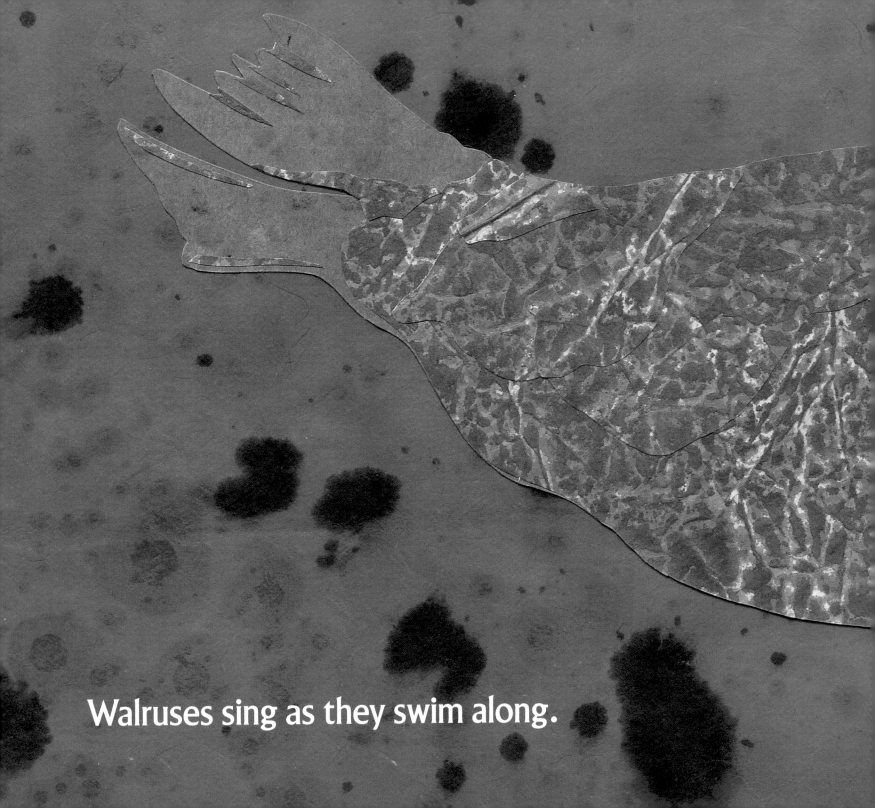

Walruses sing as they swim along.

Whales do too.

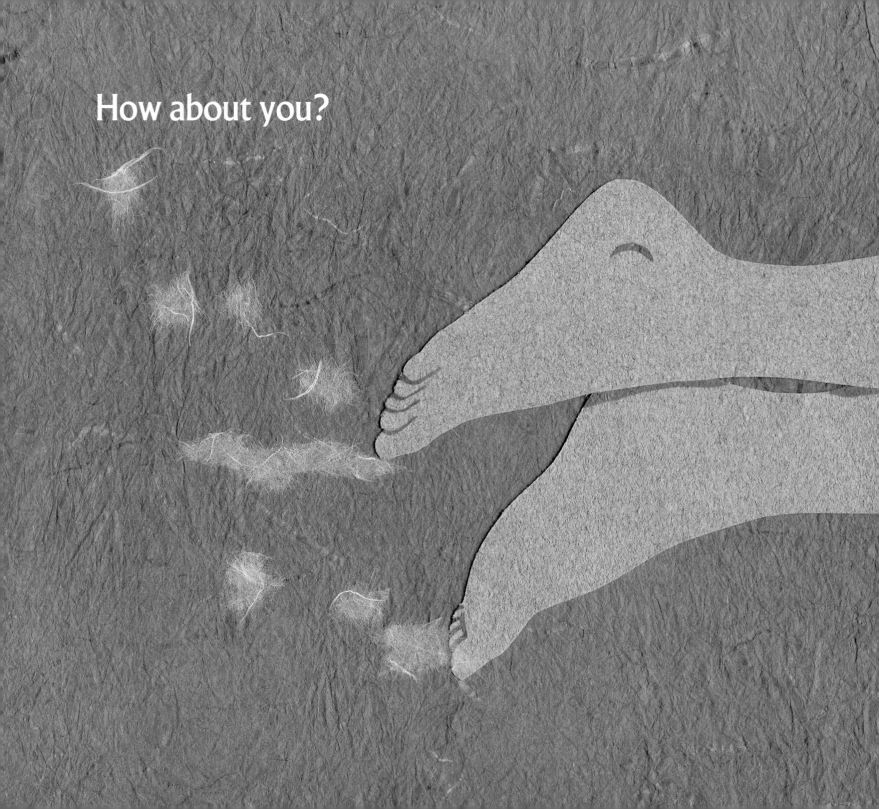

How about you?

NOTES

Elephants swim with their trunks held high.

Elephants are strong, graceful swimmers. An elephant swims with her whole body and head underwater. She breathes through her trunk, lifting it above the water like an air hose or a snorkel. In shallow water, an elephant can use her trunk to suck up water and give herself a shower.

Kangaroos swim, but their babies stay dry.

A mother kangaroo keeps her baby, or "joey," safe in her waterproof pouch when she goes swimming. A ring of strong muscles keeps the opening to the pouch closed tightly. Many kinds of kangaroos are strong swimmers and can swim all the way across a river or a lake.

Platypuses use their tails like rudders.

The duck-billed platypus uses his flat tail to steer as he paddles along with his webbed paws. When platypuses are four months old, they are about one foot long and begin learning to swim and hunt. The platypus is one of the few mammals that lay eggs.

Armadillos walk along under the water.

Armadillos often live in burrows along creeks and streams. To cross the water, an armadillo can take a breath, sink, and walk along the bottom of the streambed. Or he can gulp some air into his lungs to help him float, and paddle a short distance along the water's surface.

Tigers swim to get out of the heat.

Unlike most cats, tigers go willingly into the water. On hot days, they will back into the water, rear end first, and lie down. A hungry tiger may chase a small swamp deer into a river, then catch it.

Jaguars scoop up fish to eat.

Jaguars are strong swimmers and, like tigers, go willingly into the water. They catch and eat turtles, fish, and small crocodiles. Even when they are not hunting, they will jump into the water and splash around to cool off.

Sea otters sleep in a cradle of kelp.

Settling down to sleep, a mother sea otter wraps her baby and herself with long strands of kelp, a kind of seaweed that grows from the ocean floor to the water's surface. The kelp keeps the otters from drifting away as they sleep. When the mother wakes up, she may leave her baby wrapped in kelp and dive to the bottom to find clams to eat.

Squid swim backwards, jet-propelled.

Squid have a siphon, or funnel, that lets them suck in water to quickly fill up their bodies like big water balloons. They shoot the water out to zoom backwards, away from attackers. They can also squirt clouds of dark "ink" out of their bodies, which confuses predators and lets the squid escape.

Hippos sink to the bottom to sleep.

The word "hippopotamus" means "river horse" in Greek. Hippos spend so much time in the water that many hippo calves are born underwater. The mother pushes the baby to the top for his first breath. Hippos can sleep underwater, but they must come to the surface every five minutes to breathe.

Wildebeests wade where the water's not deep.

Wildebeests go into the water only when they must, to escape from a predator or to find food. When a lion threatens a herd of wildebeests, they will stampede into a river. Even the youngest must be ready to run. Seven minutes after a baby wildebeest is born, she can run. She must be able to cross rivers by the time she is four or five months old.

Pelicans plunge straight down from the sky.

Brown pelicans dive headfirst into the waves to catch fish. Underwater, their throat pouches open up to suck in fish and let out water. White pelicans do not dive for food. Instead, they scoop up fish with their beaks as they swim along the water's surface.

Caribou glide with their heads held high.

Caribou are good swimmers. They swim with their backs and heads above water. Their fur is made up of hollow air-filled hairs that make it easy for them to float. Like wildebeests, these "American reindeer" cross rivers in search of food.

Polar bears paddle with the greatest of ease.

A newborn polar bear is blind and weighs less than two pounds. When he is three months old, he is able to leave his den. He is soon sliding down snow banks and diving headfirst into icy pools of water. His fur gets soaked, but a thick layer of fat, called blubber, keeps him warm.

Sea turtle babies run straight to the seas.

Sea turtles leave the water only to lay their eggs. The female crawls up the beach and digs a hole for her eggs where the waves will not reach. The babies hatch at night, dig their way out of the hole, and run right into the sea. Even so, many are eaten by seagulls before they reach the water.

Walruses sing as they swim along.

A male walrus makes a beautiful sound called belling when he wants to find a mate. He has a sac inside his throat that he blows up to make a sound like church bells chiming. Young males swim in groups of four or five, practicing their songs over and over as they get ready for mating season.

Whales do too.

Male humpback whales sing songs that last as long as thirty minutes. They sing day and night, and their songs have often been heard by sailors. Humpbacks can sing the same song many times. Scientists have recorded and studied these songs. Some scientists think the songs are used to attract females, but no one knows for sure.

How about you?

Swimming does not come naturally to people. Unlike most other mammals, we have to learn how to swim. At eighteen months, a child can learn to float in the water with her legs dangling, her head held back, and her face up to breathe. At age two, she can learn to do the dog paddle. But she is not strong enough to float by lying on the surface until she is about four years old.